Nonprofit Quick Guide™

Best-Kept Secrets to Engaging and Retaining Business Donors

Joanne Oppelt, MHA
Linda Lysakowski, ACFRE

Nonprofit Quick Guide: Best-Kept Secrets to Engaging and Retaining Business Donors

One of the **Nonprofit Quick Guide**™ series

Published by Joanne Oppelt Consulting, LLC

Copyright © 2021 by Joanne Oppelt and Linda Lysakowski

ISBN Print Book: 978-1-951978-14-3

13 12 11 10 9 8 7 6 5 4 3 2 1

Printed in the United States of America

About the Authors

JOANNE OPPELT, MHA

Joanne, principal of Joanne Oppelt Consulting, LLC, is a seasoned rainmaker with a distinguished track record of success. During her twenty-five-plus years working in the nonprofit arena, she built or rebuilt successful fundraising departments at every stop, helping her organizations grow capacity and more effectively fulfill their missions.

She has held positions from grant writer to executive director at the nonprofits Community Access Unlimited, Caring Contact: A Listening Community, Family to Family Network of New Jersey, Christian Healthcare Center, March of Dimes Central New Jersey, Prevent Child Abuse New Jersey, and Maternal and Family Health Services. Her extensive background in a variety of work roles and organizations enables her to understand the realities and challenges nonprofit practitioners face–both internally and externally. Her success at every stop positions her to help any nonprofit, whether through her books or consulting practice, turn around its struggling fundraising operations.

Joanne is the author of four books and co-author of seven. She has taught at Kean University as an Adjunct Professor in its graduate program. She is also a highly sought-after speaker and presenter.

Joanne holds a master's degree in health administration from Wilkes University, where she graduated with distinction. Her bachelor's degree is in education, with a minor in psychology.

LINDA LYSAKOWSKI, ACFRE

Linda is one of approximately one hundred professionals worldwide to hold the Advanced Certified Fundraising Executive designation. Linda is the author of ten nonfiction books, a contributing author, co-editor, or co-author of nineteen others. She has also written six books in the spiritual and fiction realms.

Linda has more than thirty years in the development field. She worked for a university and a museum before starting her own consulting firm. In her twenty-five years as a philanthropic consultant, Linda has managed capital campaigns that have raised more than $50 million, helped hundreds of nonprofit organizations achieve their development goals, and trained more than fifty thousand development professionals in most of the fifty states of the United States, Canada, Mexico, Egypt, and Bermuda.

She served on the Association of Fundraising Philanthropy (AFP) Foundation for Philanthropy Board and on the Professional Advancement Division for AFP. She is a past president of the Eastern Pennsylvania and Sierra (Nevada) AFP chapters. She received the Outstanding Fundraiser of the Year award from the Eastern Pennsylvania, Las Vegas, and Sierra (Nevada) chapters of AFP, was honored with the Barbara Marion Award for Outstanding Service to AFP and received the Lifetime Achievement Award from the Las Vegas AFP chapter.

Linda is a graduate of Alvernia University with majors in banking and finance as well as theology/philosophy, and a minor in communications. As a graduate of AFP's Faculty Training Academy, she is a Master Teacher.

Dedication

This book is dedicated to all the business professionals who helped us understand their perspectives.

Contents

Chapter One

What Businesses Want

Probably the most significant principle to remember about developing relationships with for-profit businesses is that you are entering into an exchange relationship where both parties give and get something of value. It's a two-way relationship. That is, you give to them, and they give to you. You get the donation, and they get a new avenue to better meet their goals. So, to get the maximum amount of donations, you need to know what their goals are.

What are their goals? It's primarily about marketing and income. They want to increase awareness of their products and services to potential customers; in other words, increase their market visibility. They also want to expand their current customer base to increase sales and realize more profit. Businesses also want loyal customers who will stay with them and purchase their products or services again and again. They are also looking for existing customers to buy more of their brand products, optimally to the exclusion of competing brands. Companies value customer loyalty because it, like growing their customer base, leads to higher sales and bigger revenue streams. And lastly, despite common belief, most businesses really do want to be good corporate citizens. It is good for their business to have a strong community with good healthcare, wide educational opportunities, rich cultural opportunities, safe neighborhoods, and sound environmental policies. So, in the end, they benefit from a healthy nonprofit community to do this work.

It's not the gross revenue that counts in the end, though. It's net income, or revenues minus expenses. For-profit businesses, like nonprofits, try to keep expenses as low as they can. Expenses eat into net income. So, anything you can do to help them reduce costs is of value as well.

But first, you must create an awareness of your nonprofit within the business community. In **Chapter Two,** we talk at length about techniques to create awareness of your nonprofit in the corporate realm. We look at the role of targeting very specifically and intentionally and of what great value that is to for-profit agencies. We also discuss the benefits that good branding—maintaining or enhancing a good community reputation—brings to a for-profit agency.

Then you have to know how a nonprofit agency can help a for-profit organization meet its goals. In **Chapter Three**, we discuss where nonprofits can connect with for-profit businesses in meeting their goals of increased community visibility, customer acquisition, customer loyalty, and reduced costs. Again, something of great value to them.

In **Chapter Four,** we cover the six most common ways for-profits give to nonprofits. And how you can best position your nonprofit to take advantage of them. We also provide examples covering how you can shape your programming to best benefit from them. We will talk about the role of grants, employee giving programs and matching gifts, employee volunteer programs, in-kind donations, percentage of sales, and sponsorships—including other-than-event sponsorships.

Let's face it. In many ways, for-profit and nonprofits are the same. Yet, in other ways, they are different. In **Chapter Five,** we explain how to best present yourself and your nonprofit to business executives. In **Chapter Six**, we cover how to seal the deal for getting that first donation. In **Chapter Seven**, we explain common for-profit language, particularly related to marketing concepts often unfamiliar to nonprofit professionals. In **Chapter Eight**, we turn our attention to retaining the business donor and getting that second and subsequent donation.

Nonprofits and for-profits have things of great value to give to and receive from each other. The relationship will be the most lucrative to your nonprofit if you understand how you can be of value to a for-profit business, exactly how valuable your relationship is in terms of dollars, and where you can share common bonds in meeting each other's goals. Just remember that by approaching a company for a donation, you enter into an exchange relationship where both parties get and give something of value. If you just ask them to give, you will realize poorer financial results and will have missed an opportunity to garner desperately needed funds. It's a two-way relationship. Know what you have to give to the business community and how best to position yourself to realize your full financial value.

Wrapping It Up

◆ When approaching businesses, remember you are entering a two-way relationship where both parties give and receive something of value.

◆ Meeting a company's goals will help you meet yours.

◆ Businesses are interested in increasing community visibility, acquiring new customers, retaining existing customers, a strong community that results in a positive environment for their employees and customers, and reducing costs.

Chapter Two

Creating Awareness in the Business Community

The first factor in garnering a donation from a business or corporation is like any other type of donor: they have to be aware of your existence. And they have to have a way to contact your organization. So, how do you attain visibility among the business community?

Chambers of Commerce, Business & Industry Chapters, and Other Business Associations

Your local, regional, and state Chambers of Commerce, Manufacturer's Association, Economic Development Council, Business and Industry chapter, Rotary Club, and other business groups are a good place to start. Involvement in these groups means more than being listed in their directories or on their membership lists with the appropriate contact information. At the very least, you want to attend their networking events. Corporate networking events are where you get to interact with business executives, get your nonprofit's name out there, and put a face to the name. If they have an annual dinner, you want to be there, too. If they have regular meetings, you may want to consider attending so that other group members get to know and remember you.

If you want to make even more of an impression, you can join a committee or workgroup. Active committee participation demonstrates what you, and by association, your nonprofit, can bring to the table. Especially if you can bring the businesses sitting at the table market visibility, customer acquisition, customer loyalty, and/or reduced costs. You show that you not only add value to the business community, but a relationship with you adds value to an individual business. We'll talk more about the specific techniques you use to help businesses increase their visibility, acquire customers, retain customers, and decrease costs in **Chapter Three**. Serving on a committee also gives you a chance to gain exposure for your organization and cause business leaders to think of you as a peer.

One example of this was when Linda volunteered to serve on the membership committee of her local chamber. She made calls to small businesses to enlist them to join the chamber. When making these calls, of course, she always presented her business card, which inevitably caused business leaders to ask about her nonprofit. Through her involvement, she connected with dozens of business leaders, enabling her to enlist many volunteers for her annual business appeal, which you can read more about in our companion book, *Nonprofit Quick Guide: How to Run an Annual Business Appeal.*

Traditional and Social Media

In addition to networking and participating in workgroups, radio spots, TV stories, and print articles, help create community, including the business community, visibility for your agency. To target the business community, explore advertising in business publications and guesting on business-focused radio and TV programs. You can also contribute articles to business-directed magazines, newspapers, and other publications. You may even want to sponsor a business event.

To target a specific business, you can like and follow them on social media. Forward and share their posts of interest to your donors, volunteers, advocates, and community partners. Tag specific businesses as part of your social media strategy. And mention them in posts you write. Remember, they are also trying to increase their visibility. Anything you can do to further their goal will highlight your value to them.

If you're lucky, your mentions and social media posts about them may end up on the company's Intranet, where hundreds of company employees will see it, bringing your nonprofit greater visibility to a larger corporate audience.

If you are going to implement any type of business media effort, you will want to integrate your donor and agency communication efforts. If you are employed by a nonprofit with both development and communications or marketing staff, make sure you coordinate messaging and coverage and agree on which companies you will target. Resources are scarce, no matter what size your nonprofit. Leverage those resources as much as you can for maximum impact.

Suppose you are a one-person shop or have responsibilities that cover both fundraising and marketing. Rather than casting a wide net, it is best to target only a few companies so that you can actually further a relationship with them and have time to follow up. We know it's counterintuitive, but the more focused you are in your communication, the better results you'll realize. Look at it this way. Say a bullseye target represents the amount of your time and effort and the circles of the target represent the world of businesses you want to reach. The fewer circles on your target, the bigger the bullseye becomes, and your chances of hitting the bullseye increase. If time and resources are very scarce, as they are in small nonprofits, you're better off targeting particular businesses, building a good foundation, and growing slowly than trying to reach the whole business community.

Your Website

You can also draw the business community's attention by designing your website to contain keywords that business professionals may use in an Internet search. Of course, this assumes that one of the purposes of your website is to appeal to the corporate donors and that you have conducted the market research to know what words and phrases appeal to them. A simple way to conduct market research is to ask business professionals you know what language they use to research topics of interest.

So, join business associations and participate in their workgroups. Target specific businesses you want to reach as opposed to casting a wide net. Use the media to meet mutual goals. And coordinate your fundraising and communication efforts.

Wrapping It Up

- ◆ Developing relationships with business donors starts with creating awareness of your agency.
- ◆ Join your community Chamber of Commerce, Business and Industry chapter, Rotary Club, or other business or professional association.
- ◆ Get involved in committee work.
- ◆ Give business-focused media opportunities to showcase your nonprofit.
- ◆ Target specific companies.
- ◆ Coordinate fundraising and marketing endeavors.

Chapter Three

Helping Business Professionals Meet Their Goals

So, you've created awareness and caught their attention. What's next? How can you get community businesses to pay attention to you?

Help them meet their goals.

We already know their goals: increasing visibility, acquiring customers, keeping customers, and reducing costs. What are the types of things you can do to help them meet those goals?

Improving Their Visibility

How do you improve their visibility? Through your communications vehicles. We talked about using media to attract them to you in **Chapter Two**. There are other communication vehicles you can use as well. Think newsletters, email content, and social media content. For example, you can mention businesses that have supported or worked with you in your press releases. You can write an article about them to include in your newsletter. You can list them in your annual report. Other things you can do is to provide signage with their name and logo at a fundraising event, workshop, or conference you host. They can provide branded giveaways for event attendees. You can put their name or logo on your website, newsletter, event programs, or email campaign signatures.

You may be able to think of other communication vehicles you have at your disposal that can be used to help them increase their visibility. One thing we've seen was a university that ran an ad in its local business journal thanking all its business donors—receiving much better bang for its buck than expensive advertising in the local newspaper. And it encouraged businesses reading the journal to think about how they might support the university. Almost every community has a business journal. Subscribe to it. It focuses exclusively on the business community and is a great place to research the business world. You might also want to consider a subscription to the *Wall Street Journal,* especially if you target larger, national businesses.

You can also have businesses contribute to the content of your communications. For example, just as you can submit articles for their publications, you can ask them to submit articles for your publications. You can have them submit content for your social media postings, possibly boosting those postings. You can ask them to speak at one of your events. Of course, you would have to make it clear that their content must meet your approval first to make sure that you get what you need from them, not just a piece of unabashed self-promotion.

The advantage of having them provide content is that they get to interact directly with new, potential customers. Just as you are trying to develop relationships with potential customers—in this case, business donors—they are trying to establish a relationship with their potential customers, in this case, purchasers of their goods or services. The question then is, what groups does my nonprofit reach that the businesses consider good potential customers?

Expanding Their Customer Base

Companies are smart. Most of them understand that the smaller your target, the better chance of hitting the bullseye; that is, the more focused the group of potential customers they try to reach, the better they will acquire new purchasers. And acquiring additional purchasers leads to greater revenues. If your nonprofit interacts with a constituency that they want to reach, they may be interested in developing a relationship with you. The question then becomes, "Does your nonprofit interact with groups of people who are part of their target market?" And you may interact with more of their potential customers than you think. For example, if your events attract a high-income audience, maybe luxury cars, furriers, jewelers, and manufacturers or sellers of other high-end products would be a good target audience for your organization.

Think of your nonprofit's staff. How large is your staff? What are their needs? For example, if you have a large staff, they need everyday things like banking services, insurance, new or used automobiles, food, daycare, prescription drugs, and more. How do you communicate with your nonprofit's staff—staff meetings? Intranet? A for-profit company whose products or services meet these types of needs may be interested in partnering with you financially to interact with your staff.

Another constituency your nonprofit reaches is your volunteers. Like your staff, your volunteers have everyday needs. How do you communicate with your volunteers? Can you introduce them to businesses that might meet their needs?

Similarly, consider your advocates and other collaborators, as well as your donors. It might be nice if you occasionally meet their needs, as they meet yours. And I'm not talking about selling donor lists. That's a no-no unless you've clearly told donors that you periodically exchange lists with like-minded groups and offer them the opportunity to opt out of having their name sold or exchanged. What we are talking about is having a business sponsor a newsletter or volunteer event or an email campaign targeted to your different constituencies.

Businesses will want to qualify your leads; that is, get detailed information about the different characteristics each group has so they can assess the market fit. Be ready to provide information about the groups you interact with, such as standard demographic characteristics: age, gender, ethnicity, educational attainment, and income. You might also be asked about their likes and dislikes. The more specific you can be, the better your potential financial return. Remember, the more focused the target, the bigger the bullseye.

You need to know, too, what size your groups are. The bigger your focus group is, or their target audience, the more valuable the interaction with them is to the business. The key is not in sheer numbers, though. The key is the number of potential customers who would likely be interested in their products or services they can reach. The more you can qualify your constituent groups for them, the more interested they will be in partnering with you.

And don't just go after any business. Target the businesses that have something in common with you. As we have been talking about, the commonality may be a shared customer base. An example might be if you are talking to a company that manufactures toys and your constituents are mostly people with children. Bingo! - you have a match!

And don't forget about the secondary relationships. For example, does your nonprofit interact with legislators or other regulators? Company executives may be interested in interacting with them too. What kind of networking events do you offer where they both can meet?

Increasing Customer Loyalty

Not only are businesses interested in acquiring new customers, but they are interested in keeping customers. In fact, companies want to increase customer loyalty so they can cross-sell and up-sell (something you should also be doing!). And, they want customers who will buy their brand to the exclusion of all others. It is proven that customers are more likely to support companies that have social responsibility policies. For example, Linda changed her shopping habits to buy exclusively one yogurt brand, which she eats daily, based on the owner's commitment to treat his employees well and give to many charitable causes. Companies do this by associating themselves with nonprofit causes that have good reputations in the community. In other words, nonprofits with good brands. The implication here is that being a good cause is not enough. You must bring something of more tangible value to the business if you want to realize the biggest financial contributions.

Your brand awareness means knowing how many likes and followers you have on social media. And how many people in the community support your agency—such as volunteers, donors, and advocates. Who has endorsed you? What do people think of you? Just what is your brand?

In addition to your own brand followers, you can also bring value to a company through your nonprofit's operations. For example, businesses often support employee volunteer programs. What volunteer opportunities do you offer, not only that businesses can participate in, but also that they can sponsor? How do you provide services to the people you serve? How can company employee volunteers reduce your operating costs? For example, does your organization send cards to people who are home-bound? Do volunteers sign them? Can a for-profit business donate the labor and cover the costs of the cards and the mailing if you allow them to use their logo on your materials? Or can your local grocery food chain supply branded goods and employee volunteers to package them for your food pantry? Can you, instead of just covering costs, get more? It all depends on how much a target market your constituencies are. The more your market aligns with theirs, the more valuable the relationship with you.

Never underestimate how much a good market fit is worth. Businesses spend millions and millions of dollars on marketing and advertising. While you probably won't command millions, you can optimize your opportunities. Do your research first. Know your statistics. Before presenting an opportunity in final form, explore how much monetary value these opportunities are worth to your for-profit partners.

Reducing Their Costs

As in all businesses, for-profit and nonprofit, it's not only revenues or money coming in that counts. It's also the money going *out*. It is net income, defined as revenues minus expenses, that counts. High expenses eat away at profits. Companies are just as interested in decreasing costs as they are increasing revenues. So, what can your nonprofit do to lower its expenses?

We've talked at length about their visibility among their target markets. In addition to increasing sales, increasing market visibility decreases advertising costs. That is, if you can deliver on your promises. Make sure to check in regularly with the company if they see an uptick in customers due to your nonprofit's endeavors.

All companies also incur employee training costs. If your nonprofit's volunteer opportunities align with any company's skill attainment goals, you have a potential partnership. Always ask about company employee training needs to get the most out of their employee volunteer programs. For example, if education about the dangers of smoking is part of your mission, maybe you can run a smoking cessation program for the company's employees.

In addition to employee training, businesses also invest in recruiting and retaining top talent. If you can help a company attract and retain good employees, you will enhance your value to them. Association with a meaningful cause is important to today's workforce. Studies show that for-profit businesses who align themselves with reputable social causes see an increase in sales and experience less employee turnover. Like consumers, employees are more motivated to work for, and stay with, companies who do good than those who do not. In fact, some businesses limit their charitable contributions to those organizations where their employees are involved as volunteers.

All these reductions in costs point to the value relationships with nonprofits can have. When you approach a business with a potential partnership opportunity, make sure you mention the value of reducing advertising, recruiting, training, and retention costs.

For maximum donations, be creative in the use of your communication vehicles to give them visibility. Know their target market and your constituency group characteristics. Be ready to talk about the value of your brand. Point out the value of your marketing and volunteer opportunities in reducing their costs. And you will realize more revenue than you did before.

Wrapping It Up

◆ Use your communication vehicles to raise their visibility. Have them contribute content.

◆ Leverage your common bonds.

◆ Know the value of your brand.

◆ Help them reduce their recruitment, training, and retention costs using your volunteer program.

◆ Don't underestimate your nonprofit's worth.

Chapter Four

How Businesses Give

We've talked about how you can raise your nonprofit's visibility to the business community. We've also discussed ways you can help meet their marketing and net income goals, on which they spend millions of dollars. Now let's look at the most common ways businesses give to nonprofits and how you can incorporate taking advantage of their offerings through your agency's programming.

Grants

Dollars gotten that do not require a quid pro quo on your part are philanthropic dollars; that is, those donations made for charitable giving purposes. And, most often, company charitable giving means grants. Large corporations, in particular, often have company foundations associated with them. Those foundations must give away 5 percent of their corpus, just like all other foundations. When you decide which businesses you want to target, you may want to look at which ones have associated foundations. Then coordinate with your grant writer which corporate grants he or she will apply for. If you are a small nonprofit and don't employ a grant writer, you need to weigh the time investment of writing the proposal with the realistic chance of getting funded from that particular business prospect. Your chances are probably going to be higher the stronger the ties your nonprofit has with that company. For example, the company may be a vendor of yours, or you offer volunteer opportunities for its employees. To get a corporate foundation grant, you probably also need a well-developed public relations plan for letting the community know of the charitable gift. Remember, associating themselves with reputable nonprofits is a business strategy. Companies are in business to ultimately make money. If they give away money, there has to be a valuable reason why.

The downside to grant seeking is that it is time-intensive and very competitive, and usually results in restricted funding. Restricted grant funding must be used according to the terms outlined in the proposal. It cannot be used for anything else.

Employee Volunteer Programs

Employee volunteer programs are a great vehicle through which to develop relationships with businesses. As we pointed out in **Chapter Two**, nonprofit volunteer opportunities pay off for businesses who take advantage of them. As we have seen, volunteer experiences help reduce a company's recruitment, training, and retention costs. In addition, employee volunteerism is a form of charitable giving. If a company's employees are giving to a nonprofit, the company can benefit from the branding associated with a reputable charitable cause.

Volunteers Reduce Costs

One payoff for you is that volunteers help reduce costs you incur in delivering goods or services to clients. Volunteers can be used at any program implementation stage: promoting programs, gathering goods, preparing goods for delivery, or providing goods or services. In times of declining resources, volunteers can be a godsend. Just make sure you follow labor laws and regulations regarding volunteer service and reduction of paid staff.

Volunteer Time has Monetary Value

You can use relevant volunteer time as income in grant applications. Volunteer time does have a monetary value. Monetary contributions from local businesses show good community support, something important to grant reviewers.

If they fit IRS requirements, you may also be able to show the value of volunteers in your financial statements. According to the IRS, though, not all volunteer time qualifies to be listed in your nonprofit's audit and IRS Form 990 (tax return). Your auditor can give you more information about what volunteer time can and cannot be included in financial statements.

An added plus to offering volunteer experiences to company employees is the dollar-for-doer type programs some businesses have. The nonprofits receive a stipend based on the number of hours that the employee volunteers for you. This tells you how valuable these volunteer experiences are to companies.

In addition to placing volunteers in operational roles, volunteers can be used in administrative or support roles, such as assisting in a large mailing.

Clerical experiences, however, are not very valued by companies with smart employee volunteer programs. They put much more value, with the accompanying stipend, on leadership roles, such as board service.

An often-overlooked volunteer role is that of a coach or consultant. Many business professionals are experienced in marketing, branding, strategic planning, and management best practices. They may also have access to technology that is too expensive for a nonprofit to buy. Opportunities to use and sharpen those skills are valuable to companies. And you get expert advice and access to resources you don't pay a dime for.

The Nature of Volunteer Experiences

Sometimes volunteer opportunities are very short-term, one-and-done experiences, like a day of picking up trash, planting a garden, or building a home. Sometimes companies are looking for project-oriented team building activities, like organizing a food or book drive or forming a fundraising team. In our companion book, ***Nonprofit Quick Guide: How to Run an Annual Business Appeal***, we cover how to enlist business leaders in raising more money from businesses.

Publicizing Volunteer Efforts

If a company has an Intranet, this is the perfect place to submit pictures of company volunteers at your agency or with your clients, performing volunteer work. You can also submit pictures and notes from clients expressing appreciation to the company and its employees. Or post a testimonial that shows how the client's life has changed due to the company's involvement with your organization. The branding opportunities and resulting reduced costs will motivate the business to keep giving. But it is your mission that motivates the individual employees to give. Our book ***Nonprofit Quick Guide: How to Find New Donors and Get Them to Give Again*** will provide you with more insight into individual motivations for giving.

Volunteer opportunities are perfect human interest stories for use in press releases, radio and TV spots, newsletter articles, annual report content, and social media posts. Even if you can't catch them in the act of volunteering, you can still talk about what they did and tell their story of why they became involved and what they got out of the experience.

In-kind Donations

Sometimes businesses give away tangible things, such as computers, printers, or office furniture. They get the tax write-off, and you get equipment you couldn't otherwise afford. Sometimes businesses are willing to donate merchandise to a fundraising auction in exchange for publicity and community goodwill, and you get to keep the funds raised. Sometimes companies provide branded items for client use, reducing your operational costs, like canned goods, either to clear excess inventory or again, for the publicity and community goodwill. Sometimes companies provide the materials their volunteers use to carry out the volunteer activity they participate in, reducing your operational costs. In our experience, smaller, local businesses are often more willing to donate pieces of merchandise instead of, or in addition to, making monetary donations.

Employee Giving Programs and Matching Gifts

Employee giving programs are programs in which companies take voluntary donations from employees and forward them to the nonprofits they support. Sometimes companies will match those donations up to a certain amount. Companies that have matching gift programs will also match spontaneous gifts from employees (and often retirees), so be sure to ask your individual donors if their companies have matching gift programs and to credit the company for those gifts when they are received. Always ask the businesses you approach if they have employee giving programs or match employee gifts. Also, ask if there is a company Intranet where you can contribute information of interest to employees. You get excellent visibility if you are featured on a company's Intranet. It is an easy way to encourage donations. And report back on how those donations were used.

Percentage of Sales

Some companies are willing to donate to a nonprofit a percentage of sales over a specific period. This is often popular with restaurants, beauty shops, and other businesses that want to increase their traffic while helping the community. Usually, the exchange in these types of relationships is that you drive traffic to where their products are, and, in turn, they give you a percentage of sales. Sometimes you must also provide some sort of service in return, like gift-wrapping or providing information to customers. The company benefits by increasing its market visibility, acquiring new customers, and capitalizing on the branding opportunity. In addition to the financial donation, you also benefit from increased community visibility.

Sponsorships

Most nonprofits are familiar with event sponsorships. A nonprofit, however, can realize sponsorship income from more than fundraising events. Sponsorships can also be programmatic in nature. Or they may focus on your communications efforts. Or your whole agency can be sponsored. How much of what kinds of sponsorships you offer depends on your donors' preferences and what you as an organization can provide. That's why it's so important to know your constituencies' group characteristics. Make sure you take an inventory of exactly how many you reach through each different activity you conduct. If you know how many people share what characteristics, you're way ahead of the game. Because once you know that, all you have to do is tier the amount of exposure a company gets to each of its target groups to the amount of the requested sponsorship. Don't go by what others do. Know your worth and price accordingly.

Don't forget to invite businesses to the events and program activities you host, particularly if there will be legislators or industry regulators there. They will appreciate you for it.

Event Sponsorship

Break down a larger sponsorship request into parts to be allocated to different levels. For example, the lowest level of sponsorship may be a half-page ad in a program journal or playbill and an annual report listing. The next level may include a full-page ad, signage at the event, four tickets to the event, and an annual report listing. Then maybe offer a center spread ad, a banner hung at the event, six tickets, and an annual report listing. And so on, until you have everything "sold." To see sponsorship components your business community is familiar with, sign up for a business association event, peruse their sponsorship opportunities, and then go to the event to see how things work.

And it doesn't need to be a fundraising event. It can be a conference or workshop. Or even volunteer training. It all depends on the type of events your agency holds and who attends them.

Program Sponsorship

In addition to events, companies can sponsor programs. You go through the same steps as you did with the events – breaking them down into their smallest parts and then dividing them into several tiers. The most significant difference in program sponsorships as opposed to event sponsorships is the time factor. Program sponsorship opportunities can offer businesses exposure over a longer period. Investment in one-time events gets one-time exposure. Investment in a series of events, which continuous operation of a program is, gets multiple exposures over time.

Things you can do to promote your programs and the businesses sponsoring them include press releases around a mission-oriented observance for your nonprofit such as Earth Day, Suicide Prevention Week, or Women's History Month. You can also publish social media posts that feature client stories brought to you by their program's business sponsor.

If a company sponsors a program instead of a fundraising event, it is probably looking for brand visibility. Think of how the business can get brand exposure and be associated with its program over the year.

And don't think you will raise enough money to cover all your program costs. You probably won't. You wouldn't want to put all your eggs into the corporate sponsorship basket anyway. The more diversified your revenue streams, the more stable your long-term funding will be.

The advantage a program sponsorship has over a grant is that sponsorship monies can be used for anything you want as long as the terms of the agreement are met. Grant monies must be used as outlined in the grant proposal.

Media Sponsorship

You can also have what I call media sponsorships. Media sponsorships use your communication vehicles to highlight the sponsor. For example, a business may sponsor so many editions of your newsletter. Or a year's worth of interactive surveys of the month posted on social media.

Don't forget about your website and its pages. When you design or re-design your website, you can incorporate placements for sponsor logos into your design. You can have sponsors featured on your homepage or the subpages. Target businesses that have something to do with, or are somehow related to, the page on which they appear. For example, your car donation page may be sponsored by a car dealership. Or your page about your tutoring program may be sponsored by an education testing firm. If you run an animal shelter, pet food and supply companies may work for you. Just make sure that you don't waste time pursuing a competitor business, like a tutoring firm sponsoring your tutoring program.

Agency Sponsorship

You may even think of a high-priced agency sponsorship. An agency sponsorship can include any or all the components of your events, program operations, and communication vehicles. Offering agency sponsorships may be good options if you are a small nonprofit with limited staff time to pursue multiple companies or if there are a limited number of activities you conduct.

However, if you do offer multiple types of sponsorships, make sure that the agency sponsorships actually offer and cost more than lower-priced combinations. For example, you want to avoid offering a $15,000 program sponsorship that can be combined with a $5,000 media sponsorship that ends up offering the same as or more benefits than a $25,000 agency sponsorship. Your goal, after all, is to raise the most money as possible.

There are many ways for-profit businesses give to nonprofits, including grants, employee volunteer programs, in-kind donations, employee giving programs, matching gifts, percentage of sales, and sponsorships. Take advantage of as many, or as few, that your nonprofit can handle. Do remember, however, that businesses make up only 5 percent of the charitable giving pie. And about 80 percent is given by individuals. Don't put all your eggs in the corporate giving basket. Nonprofits with the most diverse revenue streams are the most sustainable.

Wrapping It Up

◆ Philanthropic dollars require the least quid pro quo on your part but are also very competitive.

◆ The use of volunteers reduces operating costs. However, be aware of applicable labor laws regulating volunteer replacement of paid staff.

◆ Volunteer time has monetary value that can be used in grant budgets. Volunteer time may also show up in a nonprofit's financial statements.

◆ In-kind donations are a common way for local businesses to give.

◆ Sometimes a company will give a percentage of sales to its nonprofit partners.

◆ Corporate sponsorships can more than fundraising events. Other types of sponsorships encompass programs, communication vehicles, and even the agency itself.

Chapter Five

Speaking Their Language

Business professionals often speak a language foreign to many nonprofit professionals. To connect with them, so they easily understand you, you need to become familiar with common business jargon. You want each side to understand the messages you send to one another.

You also want to be familiar with common business performance measures, so you know what is important to them. Knowing what performance measures they value will help you craft your offer to them. The common business term for this is key performance indicators.

Common Business Terms

Brand

A company's brand, roughly put, is its reputation in the community. That is, how the public perceives the company's products or services live up to their promises. Having a good brand means there is a highly unified, positive public opinion of the firm's products or services. Brand awareness measures how well known the brand is across a given target population. In for-profit accounting, a brand can have a monetary value attached to it. This value can show up in the company's financials as an asset and affect its worth.

Your nonprofit has a brand too. How well do you deliver services? How effective are you in meeting your clients' needs? How satisfied are your clients with your services? What level of quality do your clients expect? How do you know? What proof do you have? How does a business executive know that your perceptions of who you are to the community align with what the community thinks? Do you validate your perceptions through any type of survey? Results from community and client surveys combined with organization growth statistics can all be used as objective evidence of your nonprofit's brand value.

Market Demand and Penetration

Market demand measures how much demand exists for a particular company product within a defined target market. Market penetration measures the percentage of a specific target market that is consuming a particular company product. For-profit companies have professional marketers to help them calculate total market demand and market penetration. All you need to know is that your nonprofit can also speak to market demand and penetration, even without a professional marketer.

Think of it in terms of need. How much need exists for your nonprofit's services? Calculate rough numbers based on the needs assessments in your grant proposals. You can base your market demand calculations on the percentage of the population with the defined need. If you want to find out about needs in the U.S. population, look at the census data. If you have U.S. or state data and need local data, multiply the national or state percentage by your community's population. Yes, it's a lot of work. And, yes, it's a lot of math, and you may need help with your calculations. No, you're not going to be able to figure out a precise market demand number. But you will have an objective measure of rough market demand and something more concrete to say other than, "we can't keep up with the demand for our services." You want to ensure that the issue truly is a community need instead of bad management or inefficiencies in program delivery.

Defining market demand and penetration can help with more than just fundraising efforts. It can also inform your agency's growth and strategic plans. So, make sure to share your results with agency leadership.

Value Proposition and Unique Marketing Position

A value proposition defines the benefits a company brings to its customers. So that the product or services meet the ideal client's needs and preferences, value propositions tend to be very focused on a narrowly defined target market. Remember, businesses know that the smaller and more defined a target audience is, the greater the chance of success.

Because companies compete against other companies offering similar products, they need to find a way to differentiate themselves or stand out from the competition. The value proposition must be unique in some manner. A unique marketing position defines the benefits that the company singularly brings to the market. A unique marketing position statement is developed by looking at the value proposition in light of the company's perception of the company, the competitors' perceptions of the company, and the customer's perceptions of the company.

You, too, can develop a unique marketing position statement for your nonprofit. Capturing your value proposition and defining your unique marketing position give you a way to differentiate from other nonprofit agencies like yours. These statements can then be used as a basis for your messaging. And consistent messaging leads to strong branding. Which increases your perceived value. Which makes you a desirable partner to well-branded for-profit businesses. Which, if you play your cards right, leads to funding. You will find unique marketing position statements not only helpful in garnering business donations but also in grant writing, annual appeals, and capital campaigns.

Customer Journey and Experience

You may relate to the customer journey and experience as the donor journey and experience. Your program staff may relate to it as the client journey or experience. A customer journey, simply defined, is the culmination of steps it takes to find a company and decide to buy. A donor journey is the culmination of steps a donor makes to find you and decide to give. A client journey is the culmination of steps a client makes to find your organization and decide to enroll in services. The customer, donor, and client journeys define the pain points a customer, donor, or client experiences before deciding to proceed to the next step. Outlining the customer journey is helpful to determine when and how to reach out to your target market.

The customer experience is the series of interactions customers have with a company once they decide to buy or buy again. The donor experience is the series of interactions donors have with your agency once they decide to give or give again. Likewise, the client journey is the series of interactions clients have with your organization once they decide to enroll. You generally analyze the customer experience in terms of customer satisfaction and ease of the process. High customer satisfaction leads to repeat sales, greater market penetration, and a higher brand value. Donor satisfaction and ease of use affect the amount of your donations. High client satisfaction and ease of enrollment speak to good program marketing and rising demand for services. As you can see, outlining the donor and client journeys and experiences helps you speak business jargon and helps your nonprofit obtain more donations and reach out to your own target population.

One of the big differences between for-profit and nonprofit organizations is that for-profit businesses are generally concerned with one external target market in product delivery—the customer, whereas nonprofits have two external target audiences regarding program delivery—donors and clients.

Common Business Performance Measures

Knowing common marketing and financial measures of performance will help you better understand the business perspective, communicate your nonprofit's value to the for-profit sector, measure your own nonprofit's effectiveness, and strengthen your agency's fundraising and outreach endeavors. You can then show a company through objective data that you are moving forward as an organization.

Measures of Market Performance

Specific market performance statistics that a business executive will want to understand when determining whether or not and how much to invest in your nonprofit (think of their contribution as an investment in you) are:

- The number of event invitees and attendees;
- The number of social media likes, followers, and engagements;
- The number of website visitors; the number of unique website visitors;
- The number of people on your mail and email lists; and
- Email open and clickthrough rates.

If you will post flyers, let them know how many you will print, where you'll post, and how often you will replenish them.

In addition to the number of contacts, they will look at the frequency of contact. Don't only tell them how extensive your email list is; tell them how often you send out campaigns to specific audiences. Don't only tell them how many website visitors you get; tell them how often you update content. Do some of the math for them. Let them know how many impressions their dollar will get. Make it easy for them to see the return on their investment is high.

They will also want to know the annual growth rates of all these measures. They want to know their investment is safe and will grow over time. They want to know their relationship with you is worth the resources they put into it. If you have negative growth rates, that is, your performance has declined over time, then let them know what issues you have identified that resulted in the decline and what actions you have put in place to turn them around.

Measures of Financial Performance

Before partnering with you, business executives are going to want to see your nonprofit's financials. They want to assess financial stability. They may ask for your agency's audit or IRS Form 990. They may ask for cash flow statements. And they may want to see several years' worth. Your agency's financial officer should be able to provide you with any requested financial documents.

The business executives will be looking at net income and assets, net assets, receivables, liabilities, liquidity, and debt ratios. These values can either be found on or calculated from the numbers on your financial statements. And they will look at the footnotes in the audit. They want to see objective proof that you are as stable as you say you are.

Although knowing the ins and outs of financial statements is out of the fundraising realm (even we don't know how to calculate all those ratios), you must understand how to read and interpret a basic audit and IRS Form 990. You must also understand your nonprofit's general financial position. Understanding your agency's financials gives you a big leg up when it comes time to financial negotiations. And you will stand out from your competition. You will make a positive impression, which engenders confidence and trust, key factors in sealing the deal. Your agency's financial officer or auditor can help you interpret and understand your nonprofit's financials.

Understanding common business principles helps you and business executives reach a mutual understanding. Knowing your brand, defining market demand, developing a unique marketing position statement, outlining the customer journey, and evaluating the customer experience also helps you improve your own nonprofit's performance. To get the most money, know their priorities and what is important to them. Know how they evaluate their own performance. Make a powerful impression by speaking their language.

Wrapping It Up

- ◆ Become familiar with common business jargon to better understand the business perspective.
- ◆ Communicate with business professionals in terms and concepts they easily comprehend.
- ◆ Utilize business principles to improve your nonprofit's performance.

◆ To narrow down an agreement, know what performance measures are most important to business leaders.

◆ Understand business ideologies to boost your negotiating position.

◆ Use objective market and financial data to support your statements regarding the return on their investment in the partnership.

Chapter Six

Approaching Business Executives

So, you know what businesses want, you're networked with business associations, you've targeted some specific companies, you're meeting their goals, and you've designed your programming so that it fits into one or more of the giving vehicles. You are now ready to approach the businesses to talk about developing partnerships. In a small business, it may be simple to know who to meet with. In a large corporation, the task might not be so easy, and you may have to contact several people, one for each of their giving vehicles.

Dealing with Small Businesses

Local businesses live and die by their reputation in the community. In addition to business associations, business owners are often members of service groups, like the Kiwanis Club, Lions, Rotary, or Knights of Columbus. To meet other business owners, you may want to see if you can be invited to be a guest speaker at these groups' meetings.

In small businesses, you may just approach the owner or manager and ask how to best partner. As we pointed out earlier, small businesses may find it most economical to donate a piece of merchandise instead of making a financial contribution. If they do give a monetary donation, it will probably be small. Don't discount small contributions, though. Small donations can add up to significant amounts.

A small, local business can offer things other than money, too. They can galvanize their customers around your community event, particularly if your event is a volunteer or community organizing event that doesn't cost any money.

Dealing with Large Corporations

If you are trying to get a donation from a large corporation, you may deal with three or more people, each with responsibility for a different part of the company's corporate giving program. There are often different contacts for grants and other foundation giving, employee volunteerism, corporate sponsorship, marketing, and/or community relations arms in a large company. Specific contacts are often found on the company's website under About Us/In the Community.

Contacting Philanthropic Officers

If you are looking for philanthropic dollars, you will most probably be writing a grant or going after a direct donation. Do your research. Look at the company's website. For corporate foundations, review the foundation's 990. Find out what the guidelines are *before* you talk to a representative. Be prepared and make a good impression. Don't make the foundation representative feel like you are wasting their time, asking them questions already answered on the website.

And abide by the guidelines. Don't try to fit a square peg into a round hole. If you don't fit the guidelines, it's a waste of your time to prepare a proposal with no chance of funding. And it's a waste of their time to review it.

If you qualify, have read through the guidelines and questions and answers provided on the website, and reviewed their 990, it's time to introduce yourself to the foundation manager. If you have any unanswered questions, now is the time to ask them. Then submit your proposal and wait until you hear back. Don't call the foundation representative until you hear back from them. Only contact them when the date they said they would get back to you has passed.

Contacting Sales and Marketing Representatives

Your fundraising endeavors may help them meet their sales and marketing goals. The best entry point for sponsorships of any kind may be a sales representative, often the most visible and accessible company representative. Salespeople generally have the authority to use resources to make an immediate sale. They are focused on what is happening in the here and now. In our experience, the salesperson is the entry point to other agency executives who have a longer time frame to meet their goals. Often, the sales representative will point you to a regional account manager or director.

And those contacts are usually marketing professionals. Marketing professionals are interested in growing the company's customer base through defined target markets. They are also responsible for growing the company's brand. They are generally looking into the future. As such, their goals usually have longer time horizons to work with, giving them more flexibility to negotiate and realize results over more extended time frames.

Contacting Community Relations Professionals

Sometimes you are directed to the community relations or public affairs director. You may also come across the title corporate social responsibility manager. These professionals are most concerned about the company's image in the community. It is their job to maintain a positive company brand. They are probably responsible for managing the company's employee giving and volunteer programs. And the PR around company volunteer efforts.

Communicating with Business Executives

Whether dealing with a large or small company, you will need to develop a rapport with them. To do that, focus on what you have in common. For example, dress in typical business attire when you visit them, not in often more relaxed nonprofit work clothes. Use their language and concepts that are familiar to them and easy to understand. Don't use nonprofit jargon. Use corporate jargon instead. If you do introduce concepts they are unfamiliar with, start with what is already understood. In **Chapter Seven,** we reviewed common business language and concepts, so you don't have to start at ground zero.

You also want to match their presentation style, probably a direct, no-nonsense, get-to-the-bottom-line approach. Always be honest and straightforward. Be passionate about the partnership. Your genuineness will engender trust. Listen first. And listen more than you talk—find out as much as you can about them so that you can address their specific concerns, problem-solve with them, and come to mutually beneficial solutions.

And make sure you confirm your understanding of whatever next steps, timelines, or deliverables you agreed to. Nonprofits and for-profit speak different languages that are both English. In other words, the words you use to communicate may sound the same but mean different things to each of you. Always summarize and provide feedback on what you think you heard.

Working with Business Calendars

Your timing needs to be right, too. Although it may seem like businesses have unlimited resources, they don't. There is only so much money in the budget that can be used for any one project. This is why the more your fundraising endeavor matches their company goals, timeline, and budget, the greater your chance for approval.

Most companies operate on a calendar fiscal year. They are usually preparing budgets for the next year in the fall. Use the spring and summer to build your relationship. Then approach them in the fall with your project, but don't lead with a fundraising ask. Approach them with a mutually beneficial endeavor that is valuable to both parties. Remember, you are not asking them for a handout. You and your nonprofit can offer a lot of value to them. Don't undervalue your nonprofit's worth.

In small businesses, you may get a yes right away. In larger corporations, there is probably an arduous budget process that your contact has to navigate. You may have to keep in touch with them for six months before your project is approved. Don't be put off by the long timelines. And, unless they've given you deadlines for when they will get back to you, don't be afraid to follow up for as long a period as you need until you get an answer. Remember, you are not their primary business. You do not take priority over all the other business tasks they must get done. You are not top of mind. Your joint endeavors may slip their minds as time goes on and other things take precedence. Don't be afraid of reminding them periodically that you are still waiting for an answer. It might seem pushy to you. It doesn't appear that way to them, though.

A good way to know when to follow up is to agree on the next steps. The next step being, "when can I expect to hear from you again?" Better yet, be proactive and tell them when to expect your next call, always asking if that fits into their timeline.

And always thank them for their time and efforts on your behalf. Tell them how much you appreciate them working with you. Be appreciative of what they *can* do for you. Be a bright spot in their day. Let them know through your words and actions that you will be easy to work with and not burden them. They will most likely respond in kind.

Whether you are approaching a small business or large corporation, you need to build a relationship before agreeing on an exchange for money. Be realistic in what you can expect from them. It may take a while to communicate and hear back. Always confirm your understanding of what they expect. And come from a position of strength. Recognize the value that you bring to the table. You are not asking for money. You are asking to engage in a business relationship that mutually benefits both parties.

Wrapping It Up

- ◆ Smaller businesses tend to have less bureaucracy to wade through than larger corporations.
- ◆ Small companies are most likely to donate in-kind and make smaller financial donations.
- ◆ Large companies often have several people to contact depending on the types of giving you are pursuing.
- ◆ By word and deed, when interacting with any business, emphasize what you have in common.
- ◆ Approach for-profits from a position of strength and value.
- ◆ Always confirm agreed-upon processes, timelines, and deliverables.

Chapter Seven

Sealing the Deal

Congratulations! The company you targeted acknowledged the benefits of partnering with your nonprofit, and you're close to a deal. How do you seal it?

Make No Assumptions

First, don't assume anything. It ain't over 'til it's over. For example, they may tell you they can give you a certain donation, but it's a different story when the time comes to commit. We have seen this happen more than once. Sometimes the economy has slowed down, and the company doesn't meet or anticipate meeting sales projections. Sometimes a law has passed that will result in more industry regulation. Sometimes the budget allocations they expected didn't go through because another department needed it more. Sometimes there is a change in leadership with new priorities. Anything can happen. Whenever possible, get a signed pledge commitment, which will strengthen your position. But never assume an anticipated outcome will happen with certainty.

This means you shouldn't budget the expected donation as revenue unless the business has been steadily giving for years. Even then, expect that things may still fall through. The last thing you want to do is over-project your revenues and leave your nonprofit in the red at the end of the year. Expect the best, but plan for the worst.

Be Appreciative

Second, approach companies with an attitude of gratitude. Remember, they are in the business of making money, not giving it away. And there may be other nonprofits who have approached the company for donations that are just as able to meet the company's business needs as you. Let the company know how much you appreciate the fact that they chose to partner with you. Treat the partnership as an honor. That doesn't mean to grovel at their feet. That means that you still stand up for what you're worth, but with the full knowledge that other nonprofits can fulfill the company's business needs, too. Be grateful the company has chosen to work with *you*.

Specify and Clarify Details

Ask them, "What works best for you? Here is what I have to offer." What you're looking for is precisely how to narrow down the agreement. What elements of what you have to offer are most important to them? What can they do can do without? How important is to them that you implement certain processes? Remember to talk about expectations regarding communication processes and implementation procedures, as well as the deliverables on both sides. In fact, make the methods of delivery part of the agreement. Get agreement on both process and outcome.

Specify every detail. And clarify them. And memorialize them in writing. You want expectations to be as clear as possible. Whether you present a simple memorandum of understanding or an attorney-prepared a contract, have something in writing that you both sign and date.

If your agreement lasts for some time, have an "out" clause; that is, language that allows either party to terminate the agreement. Just in case something happens. For both of your protections. You want to cover yourself in case the relationship changes.

Command Respect

If the relationship is new, the company may want to start small and test you out before making a big commitment. As you build the relationship, you may be able to expand your mutual commitments.

Be honest and ethical. Only promise what you can deliver. Don't overpromise. You don't want to get a reputation for failure or dealing with bad faith. The money is not worth a negative reputation. A negative reputation is far more damaging to your fundraising efforts than losing a donation.

Be fair. Don't ask for the world. It may seem that businesses have a lot of money to spare, but they may not share that perspective. In fact, they probably don't. Ask them how much what you can do for them is worth to them. Do your homework regarding industry marketing and training costs. The internet is full of information. You may not be able to calculate an exact estimate of that particular company's costs, but you can get in the ballpark. If you know approximately what you're worth based on industry benchmarks, do you know how powerful that is? Not only will you be able to fairly price your offer, but you will impress the business executive you are negotiating with. You will present yourself as someone who does their homework, is thorough, and anticipates negotiations. You will be impressive. And you will command respect. Imagine what that will do for your reputation. Come in with a fair offer. Know your worth.

Never assume certain results. Budget your revenues based on what is certain, not hoped for. Maintain an attitude of appreciation and helpfulness. Specify every detail. Memorialize the agreement in writing. And be honest, ethical, and fair in all your dealings.

Wrapping It Up

◆ Final agreements may differ significantly from what was promised. Never presume outcomes.

◆ Only budget new revenues that are certain.

◆ Approach negotiations with gratitude for the partnership.

◆ Clarify expectations in writing.

◆ Knowing your worth commands respect.

Chapter Eight

Receiving Donations Year After Year

You've gotten that first donation from the company you targeted months ago! Congrats! Jump up and down and do your cartwheels. Celebrate this big milestone. Then realize life with this business partner goes on. The relationship is only the beginning; don't think your job is done. You want to be able to get that second gift next year. Maybe even a bigger gift. And maybe for years to come. You're in it for the long term. This is especially critical if you plan an annual, formal business appeal as described in *Nonprofit Quick Guide: How to Run an Annual Business Appeal.*

Communicate Promptly and Regularly

To get that second gift, you need to live up to your end of the first agreement. You need to show you are trustworthy and build on the trust so you can deepen the relationship. You need to show success.

The first thing to remember is to communicate, communicate, communicate. Just as you should with all your donors—businesses, foundations, or individuals.

The first communication should be a thank-you acknowledgment *before* the check clears the bank. Which means a quick email acknowledging receipt of the gift and a hearty thank-you for the funds.

The next step is a written thank-you letter with all the tax-deductible language in it. A hand-written note off to the side is a nice touch.

The third communication, about a week later, is an email about what has already been done to ensure fulfillment of the agreement and when they can expect to see results. You want the company to know that your agreement's fulfillment is of utmost importance to you, and you take it seriously. You also want things in writing, just in case anything goes wrong.

After that, communicate with your contacts monthly and as you hit each milestone. Frequent communication shows forthrightness and a willingness to share information. Which is essential if things go wrong or a deliverable is delayed. Just like foundation officers, business professionals don't like surprises. They have people they report to and to whom they need to justify their use of resources. Help make that part of their job easy for them.

Make sure to follow up with them once the project is finished. You want to thank them again for their contribution and include any pictures and materials that show your recognition of their donation.

And when you communicate with business professionals, be brief and to the point. Remember, you want to match them in their style.

Report on Results

And report on the results. Not only the actions you have taken required by the agreement but also your measure of market performance. As well as a thank-you for how their contribution is enhancing your mission. For example, a client story or testimonial. Or social proof of mission fulfillment, like a quote from someone in your community or a snippet of conversation overheard during a community meeting. You could also send the results of a community or client survey. Just remember, be brief and to the point.

The purposes of reporting on mission fulfillment are two-fold: 1) your mission is the crux of your brand, and they are interested in brand performance; and 2) although business executives may think of business objectives first, they are still people, and individual donors are motivated by mission. If you take this approach, you may even get a personal donation from the executive, in addition to the gift from the company. Or the executive may promote your cause to other employees, or even businesses, recruiting new donors to your cause.

Determine Their Satisfaction

Periodically ask your contact if you are meeting their expectations regarding your nonprofit's performance in carrying out the agreement. Also, ask if there is anything you can do to improve their experience with your organization. Show that you are willing to go that extra mile. Create an atmosphere of reciprocity. You want to meet their expectations so they think positive things about you and will want to continue the relationship. In addition, you don't want any surprises. You don't want to be going merrily along only to find that somehow you royally ticked them off. The only way to know for sure what they are thinking is to ask them how you're doing.

Get feedback and address any problems early, while you still have time to correct course and salve feelings.

So, communicate promptly and regularly. Thank them profusely. Report on your progress. Talk about both business and mission outcomes. Address problems early. Show them you can deliver. And then you'll be in a very good position to ask for that second gift.

Wrapping It Up

◆ Getting the second gift starts with delivering on the promises made in the first agreement.

◆ Regular communication prevents unpleasant surprises for both parties.

◆ Report on both business and mission outcomes.

◆ Ask for feedback and assess their satisfaction.

Chapter Nine

Bringing It All Together

Congratulations! You've made it to the end of the book. And what have you learned?

You know that for-profits enter relationships that are of business value. You learned that companies are interested in increasing community visibility, acquiring new customers, retaining existing customers, and reducing costs. You see how to create awareness among the business community. You understand how to use the media to meet mutual goals. You realize that to maximize your time and efforts, you target specific businesses instead of casting a wide net. And you know to coordinate your corporate fundraising efforts with grant writing and communication endeavors.

You learned how to showcase businesses in your nonprofit's communication vehicles, including press releases, radio and TV spots, newsletters, annual reports, email campaigns, social media, and your website. You recognize that to be of the greatest value and command the biggest donation, you match your agency's constituencies' characteristics to their target market. Your agency's constituencies include staff, clients, advocates, donors, and community partners. You see the importance of your brand and how a brand high value can increase donations. You also understand that you can use your organization's marketing and volunteer opportunities to reduce business costs, another way to leverage your worth.

You know the ways businesses give to nonprofits, including grants, employee volunteer programs, in-kind donations, employee giving programs, matching gifts, percentage of sales, and sponsorships. You grasp not putting all your fundraising eggs in the corporate giving basket since businesses make up only 5 percent of the charitable giving pie. And about 80 percent is given by individuals. You understand that sustainable nonprofits have diverse revenue streams.

You comprehend common business language and concepts. You also know how grasping your brand, defining market demand, developing a unique marketing position statement, outlining the customer journey, and evaluating the customer experience helps you better your own nonprofit's performance. You see how you can base an agreement on their priorities and what is important to them, illuminated in their performance measures. You understand that you make a powerful impression by speaking their language, boosting your negotiating position. You recognize the need to use objective market and financial data in your statements supporting the partnership's value.

You understand that you must develop a relationship before you can agree on an exchange for money. You know to be realistic in what you can expect. You appreciate that it may take a while to hear back from busy business executives. You grasp emphasizing your commonalities in your language, dress, and presentations. You realize you must always confirm your understanding of what they agreed upon—processes, timelines, and deliverables.

You see why you can't make assumptions regarding final agreements—business situations may change and affect a company's ability to deliver on its promises. As a result, you know to budget your revenues based on known facts, not wish lists. You realize the advantages of approaching negotiations with gratefulness. You appreciate the importance of clarifying details and memorializing them in writing. You understand the value of being honest, ethical, and fair.

You realize the importance of showing them you can deliver. You appreciate engaging in regular and prompt communication and addressing problems early. You know to report to them both business and mission outcomes. You see how asking for their feedback helps you assess their satisfaction, putting you in a good position to ask for that second gift.

That's a lot to learn. Congratulate yourself.

Know what you have to give to the business community and how best to position yourself to realize your full financial value. And come from a position of strength. Recognize the value that you bring to the table.

And know you are not asking for money. You are asking to engage in a business relationship that mutually benefits both parties. For you, that means getting the company donation.

www.ingramcontent.com/pod-product-compliance
Lightning Source LLC
Chambersburg PA
CBHW071521210326
41597CB00018B/2830